39 Social Poems

Ed Mikulski

Copyright © 2015

Bethune Publishing – The Bethune Group

Ed Mikulski Author

First Printing

All rights reserved, including the right
to reproduce this work in any form
whatsoever without written permission
from the publisher, except for brief passages
in connection with a review. Photographs may
not be reproduced without permission of the owner.
For information write: Bethune Publishing, Inc.
P. O. Box 2008 Daytona Beach, FL 32115-2008
docbethune@tbginc.org

Jacket designed by **John-Mark McLeod**

J2maginations, LLC

J2maginations@gmail.com

Book design and page layout by

Bethune Publishing, Inc.

Printed in the United States of America

Library of Congress Control Number: 2016943491

ISBN 978-0-9971548-8-7

39 SOCIAL POEMS

TABLE OF CONTENTS

	Page Number
Dedication	1
Acknowledgements	2
Foreword	3
A Lithuanian-American Easter	5
In Order to Form	6
This Poem Isn't for Posterity…It's for You	7
Passage to Anchorage	8
We All Appear to be Nuts	10
A Cat is Made for Delight	12
Actors Great	13
Christmas Eve 1961	14
1956 Tangerine Bowl	16
My Tongue Yet Ready	17
Opiniata	19
A Face at Thirteen	21
When I Was Thirteen	22
One of Us Has a Lonely Heart	23
Love for John Kennedy Toole	24
The Firmament and Those Unique Snowflakes	25
The Long and Short of a Totem Pole	26
The Answer is Three	27
St. Peter's Gate (In My Dreams)	28
On Her Bedstand	30
Just Say "No! No!"	32
Number One of All Time?	34
Two Dark Beers	35

TABLE OF CONTENTS

Where Do Kind Eyes Come From?	36
Laurels for Daytona Beach	38
For All Three	40
Back and Forth 'Cross the Rye-o Grand	41
Twelve Thousand Bad Murders	42
Fishing and Hoping	43
Two Months of No Bob	44
Ice Chips for Mom	45
As It Should Be	46
When Was I Sick?	48
That Great White Northern City	49
Judge This, Judge That	51
The School Crossing Guard	52
The Family Values Circuit	53
A Very Long Pass Into the End Zone	54
The Farmer's Garden	55

DEDICATION

This book is dedicated to my uniquely styled wife, Judi, who as her mother used to say "has always been a joy," and also "has always been a real corker." She is so true, and lucky to have been born who she is.

Such people are a reminder of how special we must try to treat all people, even when they don't act in a lovely fashion. I for one am grateful that Judi, the V.A., and others treated me so well and sometimes with true grit when my actions were anything but lovely.

ACKNOWLEDGEMENTS

I would like to thank the Live Poets of Daytona Beach for their helping me to shape my word salad into better poems. Then, I would like to thank Dr. Evelyn Bethune, of Bethune Publishing, Inc., for appearing at just the right time to publish my work….she is a wonderful speaker, author, and editor!

Also, I must express thanks to Mr. Greathouse of Cincinnati (near short-Vine) - he knows how much he improved my beliefs and attitude! And then there is John-Mark McLeod, who has done a beautiful job in designing the cover and layout of this book.

Beyond that, I would like to express gratitude for living in such a fine town as Daytona Beach; it is a little gem. There are nice friends at church and at my condo, also the clients I work with at the mental health drop-in facility – a much needed social center! I also am really fond of my friends at Oceans West – thank you, amigos.

"Just Ed"

FOREWORD

On Easter morning we altar boys rose,
clean from a gritty gray bath
after the church week marathon
with fragrant white lilies and tall thick candles.

We woke up early to starched white shirts,
stomachs rumbling from the fast,
first day again to eat chocolate bunnies
and seasonal babka and cracked colored eggs.

Linksma Diena Viespaties Prisikelimas

A LITHUANIAN-AMERICAN EASTER

On Easter morning we altar boys rose,
clean from a gritty gray bath
after the church week marathon
with fragrant white lilies and tall thick candles.

We woke up early to starched white shirts,
stomachs rumbling from the fast,
first day again to eat chocolate bunnies
and seasonal babka and cracked colored eggs.

All of our girls and ladies are beautiful today
with striking new hats and dresses,
some wearing flowers from the garden
out of black dirt moist from the March thaw.

We steered clear of the tall angry aging man
with dark black hair and fierce eyes,
his screeching voice in English then Lithuanian,
one who never smiled behind his red buttons.

We listened to the Lutheran Hour,
"Jesus the Very Thought of Thee"
after our Mass, same Jesus maybe,
then dad playing polkas on the big radio.

My father quoth "Love-Dye-Neighbor,"
which brings a smile to my face.
I guess people were more of neighbors
the farther they were from our home.

From all those years it felt like just one Easter
as we waited and hoped for different days,
and different fellows and different dads
who could actually improve on these happy days.

IN ORDER TO FORM

All eventually are folded into our America:
the black airman now allowed in a white building,
the woman now allowed to vote and to fight,
the firebrand free to pray, or not.

Even warriors without enemies are welcomed here:
the paintballers devising schemes,
and Civil War re-enactors in a 3-hour pretend spat
where no live bullets go ripping by their faces.

The echoes of real struggles thunder gently:
it was Khe Sanh and Inchon and Bataan,
and Selma and Salem and Appomattox.
We truly take pause on the 4th of July.

The U.S. stands still on this evening.
We and the bands take our seats
for the fireworks show near our Capitol porch,
then all rise for each dear one lost.

And one day there will be
health for all and a job for all,
"Afghanistan" in the past
and clean bays and rivers

If it takes all-out war to get there
in our beautiful country worth fighting for
and having it out with the next band of aggressors,
then to rest on these days of peace.

THIS POEM ISN"T FOR POSTERITY...IT'S FOR YOU

Does this poem remind you of your
smoldering teenage crushes?
Is it kind of like your first king crab legs
with drawn butter?
Is it sounding better than
"See the Pyramids Along the Nile?
Does it twist the same as Shakespeare?

Is it more comfy than your favorite book
you've ever read?
Better than the birth of your son?
Better than the thought of salvation?
Better than those steaming woolen
mittens with ice chunks?

Better than your mother's love?
Better than "Rhapsody in Blue"?
Than a song and voice that chilled your spine?
Than hearing there's no one like you,
in a good way.

Than finding a five dollar bill on the street?
Than that film that so touched your heart?
Is it better than at least a few of those things?
Nah, I didn't think so.

So, as some might say
If this poem isn't any better than that,
If it isn't any good at all,
Have Fido cover it with yard dirt.

PASSAGE TO ANCHORAGE

When we came to the end of
our seven days, the survey said
they hoped our cruise on this giant
had gone alright.

For a week we had seen
endless Alaska mountains
rising out of very cold water
and passing steadily behind.

We landed in the wonderful
little town with even a thrift store,
and a bridge with many salmon
below and seals feeding.

On the opening day we had sailed
right past the Vancouver park at dusk,
just clearing under the bridge
as cameras flashed and locals waved.

The crashing of the glaciers
named after Yale and others
broke the stillness, pushing glassy waves
under smallish cold ice floes.

We were haunted then in 2003 by the
new Italian tenor for the first time,
played mah jongg, and heard accents
from all over the world.

So yes, we did love our cruise on this big ship
that had to first squeeze through Suez,
too big for Panama, with officers and crew
from Italy, England and 39 other countries.

We loved being treated like royalty here
on our first such excursion, though one of us
was the son of a Scranton laborer,
and the other from somewhere like Hicksville.

I did wonder, though, about that
diabetic woman who demanded
early boarding to eat, and
keep from fainting.

How many bowls of chow did she finish
off that day to preserve her health?
What did her survey say when those gates
finally closed on her butt?

But still, the ship had met most everyone's
highest hopes, including mine for those
belly bloating buffets.

It was luxury treatment,
right up until our cruise cards were
powered off, making room for
the next group to crush in through the gates,
for just a little lunch.

WE ALL APPEAR TO BE NUTS

Dear sports fans:
Do your gyrations
in front of the T.V.
help your team win?

Dear bowler:
Did your body English
keep the ball
from landing in the gutter?

Dear lottery player:
Is playing all your
family's birthdays
a solid financial plan?

Dear announcer:
Do you "jinx" the pitcher
by mentioning he has
a no-hitter going?

Dear smoker:
Does lighting your ciggy
at the bus stop
make the bus come?

Dear grocery shopper:
Does your appearance
at Line 2 make Line 3
speed up before Line 2?

Dear suede-o intellectual:
Does my 115ish I.Q.
make my judgments
superior to the 150's?

Dear movie goer:
Did your rooting for
blind Audrey Hepburn
help her escape Alan Arkin?

Dear doubter of everything:
Can you act like the above, and
still be convinced you're right?
Like none of this empathy matters?

A CAT IS MADE FOR DELIGHT

One foot two, no more than that
Peeper was my loved tuxedo cat.
Jenny chose him for us one Christmas
at the pet shop on the short-Vine isthmus.

He learned to love us, but love came slow
After two years under the porch he'd go.
Kids came by to ask for "Peeda,"
and he loved to hang out by Charlita's bird feeda.

What mind was behind those cuckoo eyes
that taught me his preference in cat food buys?
With total strangers he'd walk the road
but for six years where did he unload?

As Peeper lingered, it taught me that
pure love is tender, for even a cat.
This sympathy God must have, and then
the miracle of life plays over again.

ACTORS GREAT

As with Shakespeare, there is
a notion about speaking in formal tone,
most preferably with British
or pseudo-British accent.

Old actors sounded so quippy
to themselves, so don't forget
the high-class staccato of
Reginald Van Gleason the Third

Or the Locust Valley lockjaw
of Thurston Howell the Third,
or the lovely Philadelphia style of
Louis Winthorpe, another Third.

You get mileage from a British accent,
whether it's real or phony.
It even helps to speak this way
when you are selling baloney.

CHRISTMAS EVE 1961

On December 24th our family knelt and prayed
each in a corner of a warm room
then gently passed a communal meal
of whiting and red macaroni.

We donned then our coats and collars
in our 60 watt lit living room
with Christmas tree in full dress
and fragrant smell of spruce branches.

We walked out on snow
that squeaked under each step
and a few big snowflakes fell
on a windless, wondrous night.

Our church steeple and rows of houses
stand stark against the distant hill
somehow knowing what night it is
on the dimmed light of Christmas Eve

In church we still are bundled up
with noses cold, cheeks red,
eyes blinking from seeping emotionless tears,
and boots dripping on the cold green and black floor.

At home it's the season of filberts
and Brazil nuts and bitter bits
in pecans and selecting chocolates,
and tangerines in stockings,
even awaiting the Tangerine Bowl.

It was Lionel trains and
toy conductors and station men
swinging out and waving their lanterns
toward electric-smelling tracks.

It is only a priceless dream
of life most gently lived
regardless of any presents
but deep and secure in love.

1956 TANGERINE BOWL

The Hillsdale College football team
blew their chance for the usual maniacal
sports nuts' praise.
Can you say "kudos?"

They declined a bid to the 1956 Tangerine Bowl.
Their two black players were (prayerfully?)
invited to not come, instead to stay in Michigan.
And all God's people said...?

The game was played in Orlando.
The all-white final score was:
Juniata 6, Missouri Valley 6.
There were some equally ridiculous
all-white basketball games that year too.

But by 1956, Bill Russell, Rosa Parks
and the Supreme Court were also moving.
Things have gone forward since then,
other than the Supreme Court part, which
at times has been no more supreme
than a pizza pie.

MY TONGUE YET READY

As young men we stood and shivered
while the boot camp instructor
pondered his next move.
We were lean and it didn't matter much
when the next meal was coming.

Our opinion didn't much matter either.
In fact, our opinion did not exist
as we tried to keep up,
and survive the next onslaught.

Now, a pound a year later
I can no longer keep up.
And my stomach as big as my chest was,
and my legs the size of a waist.

I'm carrying a 25-pound bag
of dry cement on each shoulder,
and the only thing that has kept pace
is my now-opinionated tongue

I'm no longer a Vietnam-era vet,
but a Vietnam vet.
I drink beer down at the local hall
And give almost one percent to charity.

I help the hungry one day a year.
Guess which day?
And I resent today's poor, who are not
as worthy or photogenic as the
Great Depression soup line poor.

Thank God my education and health care
are already grandfathered in.
Otherwise, how could I afford, rising each year,
$20,000 for full health care and $40,000 for college?

So now let the young have their day.
Let them compete against the new odds.
They could do it if they weren't
just so darn lazy, and just not as good.

With my huge stomach and
skin now brown and hair white, reversed,
I know the new world would love to hire
someone who earned it all on their own,

Someone whose slow knees
scream from pain, but
whose now-fast mouth chants:
"Me me me me me."

OPINIATA

I am like a yo-yo,
Not Christian, not Jew.
Comfortable Income, Great Education!
Bookstore Lover!

Eighty years ago, my intellectual forebears
Studied bare-breasted tribes;
They kept a straight face; they sent pictures back.

I love churches too, though not as much as
bookstores;
I go there to observe
Other people's views,
If not Christian, not Jew.

Observing,
That's what I like,
If the atmosphere's controlled,
If the atmosphere's white.

Eating healthy, hypomanic smile always,
With my Bermuda shorts and neat black socks.
Listening to the views of witches,
Of Indians, of proud atheists, of
Quaint believers from foreign lands.

Myself not really believing, but ever
Ready to share
My opinion about this.

Looking in all directions first,
Smiling and head bobbing towards really no one.

Then, giving my opinion last
And foremost. Listen up!
I celebrate life.
For when I die, I'm going nowhere,
I opine.

A FACE AT THIRTEEN

Red bullets of grease
Swell up then mightily explode
One on top of the other,
Ruining a debut.
Big bumbles on cheeks,
Over a bloody terrain,
Black-tipped stovepipe
Mountains and valleys
Stand dead.
Reddened skin comes to a boil,
Running down to my neck
Now adorning,
With squinted eyes
And my arms aside
A perfect scream.

WHEN I WAS THIRTEEN

When you are thirteen
you don't have a say.
You get a chocolate bar
and some potato chips,
and the next day greasy pimples.

They are on your chin,
and it takes you a while to really
disagree with their saying pimples
have nothing at all to do with food.

Later these were upgraded to "zits."
But mine were all-too-familiar
sore red pimples that made me so ugly,
though the experts didn't really care.

I had nine cavities from soda and
almost no brushing.
One bath a week, greasy hair too,
but never thrown in the tub
by those who should have known better.

The pimples angrily explode
on top of one another.
Dark-rimmed Frankie C. had so many,
and very big ones too.

I remember his face,
with big bumbles
and tooth braces also.
He grinned and didn't seem to care.

But for years I dreaded those pimples
and wiped the wet round pads.
Disgusting was how I felt.
I blame my 1950's caretakers, yes and no.

ONE OF US HAS A LONELY HEART

I met my friend in Cincinnati, but he had been
hoping for something else. So he went to the
ward restroom, and on both knees questioned
why someone so angry had been sent.

Slowly we became friends, and
talked often about the kind man
I could become, if I would only
follow these main points.

I followed them, and minor miracle
to me, became that happy person.
I would finally not look to others for
praise, knowing that I had a friend.

Years passed and I moved, and
as it happened, I am the one with the
lonely heart. I could not understand
his choosing others over his sidekick Ed.

Now without Brandon, I was a leftover
to find another. There is still one friend
in the mirror – my ultimate approver, and
there's another friend on the other side.

Yet ever a people seeker, I tried busywork jobs,
and sampled fraternal, poetry (ha ha),
sports and church groups,
even one group for streetwise strugglers,
forced to choose one addiction over another.

Left behind by my first friend, after much searching I
found the group that loves me as I love them. A truly
accepting community of stable mental health clients,
just like me. You can cut the love with a knife.

39 Social Poems — Ed Mikulski

LOVE FOR JOHN KENNEDY TOOLE

Were you quiet then
as you're silent now?
Did your mother love you always?
Did she love a little Johnny?

Did you spin your way through high school?
Were you ranked as number one?
How did you become so heavy?
Were you ever having fun?

Did Fortuna send you to Tulane?
Did a circle start to form?
Did you seek the comfort of "other love?"
Or could Pliny keep you warm?

In the days before Matt Groening,
did you seek to be top-hundred?
Did the critics ever miss a thing,
when circling with their pencils?

One hundred years hereafter
with the dirt on all our graves,
Are you important now that you are "Toole,"
Does it matter anyway?

Is your book then just a tschotchke
on the shelf of some future son,
like a family Bible collecting dust,
never read by anyone?

What is your legacy, Johnny,
now published everywhere?
Was it that you made top-one-hundred,
or that you made somebody care…?

Speaking of numbers, what are the odds
you'd land in the city of Emeril?
In 2080 are you still "loved Johnny,"
or was your book just that ephemeral?

THE FIRMAMENT AND THOSE UNIQUE SNOWFLAKES

Our sky is made of endless miles of space
13 billion light years at last count
and this is just a part of the amount
that dwarfs all things about the human race.

By contrast earth has just begun its chase
and 30 thousand feet the highest mount
so miniscule a portion from God's fount.
Space minus four hundred plus degrees, dead place.

But earth is quite important, filled with love
and roses, painted sunsets, family poses.
If men should trip should we give them a shove?
Does it matter if we sucker punch their noses?
Is earth's path really guided from above?
And should we care about the words of Moses?

THE LONG AND SHORT OF A TOTEM POLE

Layered on a totem pole
is not a quaint mystery
but a local history
with the image of a bear, topped by
a raven, a frog, a Tlingit, and a double eagle.

But on top of this totem
in the pioneer square,
the pioneer governor from his topmost perch
peruses the land he took from
the original Americans, with violence.

His head is permanently hatless.
He looks out through the fog
and through the rain
and then with Christmas snow
atop that doe-eyed wooden head.

But most frequently of all,
through the skill of the carver,
seagulls land on the hatless pate
and leave the Tlingits' comment.

So here is yet another man who thought
he could get away with stealing
a beautiful piece of land,
even selling it to a later invader.

Seward's folly,
sic semper tyrannis, ecce babulus.
The only defense against a perfect tyrant
is to tell the Alaskan history in very short,
not long, form.

THE ANSWER IS THREE

So how many
battalions are there
in a regiment
of 2,000?

And how many
regiments are there
in a brigade
of 6,000?

Or how many full
brigades might there be
in a division
of 20,000?

A dead brother I knew was
in the 3rd battalion 82nd artillery
of a brigade in his "Metrecal,"
really Americal Division.

How was it in his
"Sunny Bietnam" for one year?
The letters to his mother never
seemed to let on.

From a distance, seems now
like it wasn't a cool "ready, aim, shoot,"
where the surprised foes never shot back.

That scene would have been
much prettier for our loved ones
than the 50-50 odds they faced,
many of those 365 jungle nights
and days a year, against the lobbing,
firing, swarming Viet Cong.

ST. PETER'S GATE (In My Dreams)

They all met at St. Peter's gate
hoping to enter in,
each one shouting their argument
O what a cacophonous din!

"Me-Me-Me" clamored the crowd,
shoving aside the fate of all others.
In this crunch-time crowd of men
no one was seen as a brother.

Like the wizard Peter gave his decree:
"Go back to Las Vegas" he stated
"where your odds of entering will be assessed,
and by impartial oddsmakers rated."

Week after week Vegas gets it right,
when competing teams think they're great.
But only one of each two is the winner,
and having just as many losers, just fate.

So: 100 average I.Q. of each selfish group:
All have equal odds!
Seldom changing their brainwashed childhoods:
Equal odds! All disrespecting others'
equally culture-bound beliefs: Equal odds!
And thinking the deity is meaner than they are:
Equal odds!

Off to the side from this ugly clamoring "Me-crowd":
Left field: the Crocodile Hunter;
Center field: Pope Francis,
Right field: Soldiers; Third base: Jesus Christ;
Shortstop: Pee Wee Reese (look it up);

39 Social Poems — Ed Mikulski

Second base: Your mom;
First base: John F. Kennedy;
Pitcher: Martin Luther King;
Catcher: Yogi Berra. Relief pitcher:
The one who created pi and the galaxies;
The fans: all who "pull" or pray
For another being in distress.

39 Social Poems   Ed Mikulski

ON HER BED STAND

B ayonne, New Jersey is my home town
E xcellent city to be from;
A ll the good times in New York
U ntil 4 A.M. we'd play and work.

T he whole gang met at Blanche's place
I n winter we danced on Fridays;
F elt like we owned this beautiful world
U ntil World War II and cry days.

L inden outings, Asbury trains
M any good times after the war;
E ven Columbus, Ohio was young and green,
M aking 25 years of being on scene.

O nce married life for others began
R eally liking being a mother;
I n my heart a love that's pure, for
E d and Tony and their father, "The Other."

S ewing and washing and cooking and feedings,
N ice Sunday dinners and Christmastime greetings.
I guess when Minnie and Mike went away
C areful thought was needed, but I would stay.

E ddie was good at all the sports,
F rankly at schoolwork too,
U ntil he ran into I'll not tell
T hen he learned to stand up and rebel.

U nreal love I've had for my sons,
R eal love for great times and great people;
E d says my best years are yet ahead
Y et not under any church steeple.

E ddie is a great Number 2 son of mine,
    but if there's a heaven, my Number 1
T ony is with God divine.

JUST SAY "NO, NO!"

A t the unripe age of ten
I n the quiet of her room
L ittle girl unprotected
E xpects a coming doom.

E ntering her privacy a second time
N ow she knows what is expected.
W ill he smile as he takes his turn,
U sing her as he directed?

O nce it's done his mind deflates,
R olling around she cries.
N ow it's a pattern she's coming to learn
O nce the pain and the swelling subside.

S choolwork just doesn't seem the same.
S eems her friends they all have changed.
H ow could they know what she's been through?
O nly she knows when hell-time came.

U sing her key she enters the house,
L acking appetite for dinner.
D oesn't eat, she's not so hungry,
H ow could she be like others, a winner?

A ll the nights right through the summer,
V ery hard to sleep.
E very day she has day-mares,
J ust in her heart, no treasure to keep.

U nless she's turned to alcohol,
S he wouldn't know any salvation.
T here grew in her heart already a hole.
S he felt just devastation.

A t the ripe old age of thirteen,
I n the course of just three years,
D elicate face with neat, thin lines

N ow looks like a light-stricken deer.
O ver and over she lives the same rapes,
T hen over and over again.
O ur yet-pretty heroine emptily smiles,
R eliving confusion and pain.

E ver since then, she's not the same,
V ery few things interest her.
E very once in a while something new comes along,
N ovelty stunts, or cool rock song.

G et over it, little heroine.
E very day I'm glad I wasn't you.

NUMBER ONE OF ALL-TIME?

Hard Iron Mike is a terrifying hitter.
He seems in no way an underdog.
He's the last guy you'd want to meet,
on the other side.
Outside the ring he's just another citizen
That had a frightful upbringing.
But he survived the mean streets.
The meanness rubbed off on him.
The meanness rubbed off on others.
Inside the ring, he's not a very nice guy.
He's the guy you'd want, if it was your chips that were down.

He's the guy you'd want, if it was your chips that were down.
Inside the ring, he's not a very nice guy.
The meanness rubbed off on others.
The meanness rubbed off on him.
But he survived the mean streets.
Outside the ring he's just another citizen
That had a frightful upbringing.
He's the last guy you'd want to meet,
on the other side.
He seems in no way an underdog.
Hard Iron Mike is a terrifying hitter.

TWO DARK BEERS

Two buddies
out of their car
walk into a dark bar
"How much for two dark beers?"

"Two little beers,
or two bigger beers?
You have that choice,
and I will serve you."

"Is it sweet then to the tongue?"
asked the bigger of the buds.
"No, it is bitter as the bitten pip.
It is warm yet boldly bitter beer."

"Two big bitter beers then,
as bitter is best,
and bigger much better yet
to lather the back of my throat"

So two buds drank
a bitter feast
of bitter hops and gathering yeast.

WHERE DO KIND EYES COME FROM?

He always had kind eyes,
and when we checked him in
to his first day at the nursing home
the staff member commented
on what a nice guy he was.

My wife and my mother both
held their hands and their purses
zipped together in their laps.

I never left visiting Dad
for the seven years he was there alone.
During Ivan I saw him for the last time,
though the actual day he died
the road up to the mountain home
was being washed out.

Years earlier I had tried to
help him out as he tended his garden,
holding his weight up as he leaned
to the left on his converted broomstick.
His response to my offer:
"Because ya can't!"

The day I graduated high school
was just enough evidence to me
 that everything would be alright.
If I just outworked everybody,
then there would be enough talent there,

Despite what my father told me what
my mother had said, about whatever will be,
and who would or wouldn't make it in life.

The first and last time I packed my bags,
I was three years old, and remember well
my father laughed as he predicted I would not
 get farther than the hundred feet or so
to the railroad track.

That time he did not mock my sobbing with his
imaginary violin, playing and singing
"Dee... Roodily Doodily Doodily Doo!"

Many times later he would
play that air violin and sing to me
but I would not leave again,
despite at least two offers.

In fact, I felt sorry
for Pat and Dennis,
whose father was an alcoholic
and beat them.

I did not leave my father,
though I have not cried
the tear I hoped I would shed.
No doubt a lot of me got shut down,
though I always would deny it.

I did learn why to care,
and have my own kind eyes.
I so learned to cry,
but as fate would have it
not for him.

LAURELS FOR DAYTONA BEACH

Daytona is a small city of 65 thousand
that is yet home to women's golf,
stock car racing, Bike Week, Biketoberfest,
a spring break, and Turkey Run.

And in a tiny waterbound area,
a great little library,
a palm tree lined ballpark,
and a friendly farmer's market.

There are boats and water, manatees, fish
and dolphins, bandshell concerts at the shore,
and courteous drivers that fill the center lane
six-deep, so that just one can turn right.

Swimming is warm for eight months,
but it's amazingly cool in this blue-collar paradise.
The gem of an airport has one gate, Gate 3,
close by our only mall, accessed by sleepy Dunn.

With living costs so low, you'd think
this beach town would be
up north, like some 90-minute stressful commute
refrigerator city, where they have four seasons but
count them, five cold months of cloudy chill.

But the tough thing about Daytona is:
when it's warm
you must jump in the pool,
or the 80-degree ocean, then not towel off.

Once the fleas were eradicated
and air conditioning invented,
our city fathers had a dream,
and do our city sons dream now.

These sons' new dream is that we should pay
a manager to neuter that tiny area downtown
so we can measure up to some
chilled Homeville up north that does not have:

1 beautiful ocean
2 seasons – summer and spring
3 colleges for our 65,000 people
4 good farmer's markets

5 in-town golf courses
6 miles of sailboat views
7 special event weeks
8 months of beach weather

9 innings of minor league shenanigans
10 in the morning salt air breezes
11 waterfront fish sandwich places, and a
12-minute drive to everywhere good.

There's a 13-hole short golf course,
and now 20 not 14 million visitors every two years.
Need we pay a manager to up that to 21 million,
compared to so few touring those Homevilles?

FOR ALL THREE

We went to Alaska
and saw the salmon run:
Five kinds, like five fingers
on an upheld hand.

We know the bears feed off of them,
as do fishermen, with families to nurture.
And there were friendly native townspeople,
and picturesque eagles, snow caps and whales.

The trip back south was by boat,
with more nature and beauty to see,
remnants of the overharvest of otter skins,
and the Pribilof Islands seal massacres.

We heard one of the tourists yell
"Yep, there they are,"
informing us hopefully more naïve others
of a "Watch this!" moment for them to share.

Well for all of us, it was really only
a few moments in four days to be whale huggers,
and the very little that means, sandwiched
between twelve greasy fork-to-mouth repasts.

What did strike home was the remarkable
countenance of a now quite fat young man
wishing for a different life, and the evenly-timed
strikes on the floor of an angry lady's metal crutches.

Also, the echo of a young girl's words:
that she had cried every day of
her first three weeks of boarding school.
What love could make a difference for all three?

BACK AND FORTH 'CROSS THE RYE-O GRAND

Native Americans roamed the land.
and our country was their land
from California to Alaska,
from Dakota to Manhattan island.

We fought them at the Alamo,
and drove them back to Mexico.
No mercy on the Sioux,
no mercy on the Aztecs.

Their bodies could not resist the
strains of disease that entered in.
Their buffalo, shad, and salmon were killed,
and the decimated remnants became ours.

We had such a need for Lebensraum
that no one could contain us.
Buffalo soldiers were added to the fray,
and profits grew like Topsy.

Now the Aztecs are trying to take back
their land across the Rio Grande.
Border guards may catch them anew, and
Keep our red, white and blue from former natives.

So as they try to re-enter the land of the braves
the Aztecs and redskins are the bad guys again,
and our enforcers will make these tyrants tremble
for challenging the red, white and blue.

TWELVE THOUSAND BAD MURDERS, BUT SOME QUITE NICE

Well, if you called America a war zone,
There'd be 12,000 mostly handgun murders a year.
The inner-city ones sure are bad.
And how about those husband and wife murders?
Lots of them, and just about all of them bad.
But the good murders are just so romantic!
What ho, murder most divine!
A foggy night, a rich setting,
And characters just pretty enough
To be snuffed in dime, now 10-dollar novels.
Slam those books down
Like any gourmand at a free buffet.
One after another after another.
After all, reading is good for you.

FISHING AND HOPING

She stands at the edge of the ocean,
a seashore full of fish,
hoping to catch a nice one or two,
oh that would be her wish.

To catch a big fat redfish
or maybe a mess of blues,
and that is why she's wading forth,
having slipped out of her shoes.

The cast is far, she settles back,
the sand between her toes,
as schools of pelicans glide the waves
before hopeful Jills and Joes.

The sky is extra blue today,
the wave heights are just right,
the shrimp and mullet are on the hook,
as she waits for that first big bite.

The tug it comes at just the right time,
before half an hour had passed.
It is a very beautiful time,
her first of this year, but not her last.

TWO MONTHS OF NO BOB

We tried a little
to meet without you.
The calendar passed by
but there was no first Wednesday.

There was no smiling face,
no skillful hands,
no word conductor
mildly praising our work,
while somehow scaring off
all the bad poets.

Glenda said
"To heck with it,
I'm not coming back in October,"
but she's here to say
hello to you in November.

Ed and Alice met once.
It was 15 minutes and one
short poem,
then we talked about Bob
and how much we missed him.

So welcome back, Bob.
You are pulling for us.
We will try harder
to make poetry
that will bring more smiles
to that wonderful face of yours.

ICE CHIPS FOR MOM

Her hand for the
first time ever
reached for mine
and confidently held it.

In June of '03
I got the call
on Route 84
Mom going to hospice.

Her weight went up,
her weight went down
with water weight
and water pills, many water pills.

The head nurse said she gained
due to overeating,
but my eating her breakfasts
did not make me gain.

I seeped warm tears
for minutes at a time and
watched the machines slowly
register her low vital signs.

The doctor teased
that the P.A. always had
the weepy effect
on people.

I took Mom to the window
to see the light
but she said really don't bother,
she could not see the shapes.

But she was there
in the room
to see me
before she went.

AS IT SHOULD BE

He always knew that he'd be great.
He wet the bed till he was eight.
He hogged the candy from a spelling bee.
No common boy was this, thought he.

Caught cheating on a high school test,
not expelled and marked, at the teacher's behest.
Disgust and pity crossed the teacher's face.
The Lithuanian genius' first taste of grace.

"Crazy Eddie," Strange," "Pope Vert the Fat."
He'd still win out, despite all that.
Potential greatness to be discovered some day,
though stuffed in a dumpster in a drunken fray.

He smoked like a fool, with panda eyes,
frozen by substances, depression, bad highs.
Body self-attacked, out of breath.
Feels like drowning, not feeling death.

Next atheist thoughts, vehemently strong.
He looked in the mirror all hour long.
Picked at himself, though no one could see.
Raged at his wife at 23.

Achievements still eluded him,
excuses now becoming thin.
Some if they knew would get even with Ed,
but he smiled and to the great day he sped.

His course, he thought, would upward lead.
Second divorce, a mistake, but with lesser speed.
Alone with his Kessler's and lottery tickets.
A memory now his human rights pickets.

"Worthless" cried his father then,
"I knew it would be since you were 10."
Death of his Tony, but did he care?
Was there any concern for others there?

Wrinkles streaked the panda eyes.
To change the real world, many lies.
"I'll write the great novel," his next refrain.
The chosen one will write of pain.

The great work stopped at Page 18.
Painful, sophomoric, what talent seen?
X-wife, X-dog, X-house, X-son,
X-dreams were felt at 41.

Gray hair crossed his wrinkled brow.
What greatness would he seek for now?
Out of sync, and out of step,
potential still within his grip?

All else had failed what he'd become,
A sickboy with a crooked thumb.
No golfer great, this man doth smell,
still striving for a polished shell.

By grace not taken at 43,
I looked at what had become of me.
A saint or angel God had sent,
before all life and talent spent.

Sold to anger, lost to pride,
I finally looked to the other side.
The sweet lord came and died for me.
All pride's in Him, as it should be.

WHEN WAS I SICK?

The doctors gave me
a serious health diagnosis.
It was so bad that
my girlfriend left me cold.

My countenance was drawn and scared
so they hid their children behind them, and
avoided words beyond "We missed you last Sunday,"
because I might throw up in their car.

And since I had not signed up for big quarterly fees,
the charges piled up, with just one do-no-harmer
actually depleting my future,
collecting whether I won or lost.

And those who love enchanted mankind
but run out of patience for one as pitiful as me
looked down to their stylish watches and said:
"Would you look at the time!"

And those who love all womankind did only that
because, beyond twenty five bucks an hour
plus prepaid health coverage, they are to me
as they have brayed: "a fish without a bicycle."

And so be it. There was just one lovely friend
who, like Seth, stuck through with me
without payment, without agenda,
with nothing, not even a prayer.

THAT GREAT WHITE NORTHERN CITY

So lots of people move the Bekins
from Chicago down south.
But why do 98 per cent of those trucks
deadhead empty back to Illinois?
Well, the southern retirees are not going to
pay big money
just to gawk at the jimmy crab skyline
of some cold place they don't know.

By crack, it's a fighting, chippy Big Julie's
city on the lake,
which Second City has the proudest citizens
in the world.
But for three months Tom guesses when the temp
will get up to 32,
and for three months the slush piles
are whipped solid by the hawkish wind.

But this just isn't any quaint amblin' ramblin'
happy wanderin' number two place,
like one guy painted, only full of simple-minded
eastern-European Yoshko's, sittin' under a tree,
eatin' kielbasi, playin' da 'cordeen, and just giddy,
slavin' six elevens in Upton's jungle.

Yet some of da Bears fans do retain an eyaccent,
even 'dough dey don't tink so.
Dey send "tank you" cards, just as rough
Scrantonians like me do. But Chicago,
being quite diverse, also has its share of vegan, tree-
huggin' gluten pukers.
Any accent they have is reserved, or they might
sound a bit like New Yorkers.

So here's the thing: you too can hire a van
and search for happiness
by moving to a place that's 10 degrees warmer.

39 Social Poems   Ed Mikulski

But then there would be no
Royko, no Wrigley, no Belushi's,
no deep dish, no Vienna dogs, no Blackhawks,
no Sox, no Bulls, no Pier or river, no Loyola,
no loyalty, no Mr. Banks.

JUDGE THIS, JUDGE THAT

Come unto me, murdering Paul,
and Peter who denied Christ and cut off an ear.
Come unto me with broken heart
except if you love your beer.

All ye that are heavy laden
like Bathsheba's second husband,
come to a stiff-necked judging church
where faults are denied by the dozen.

Moses murdered the Egyptian man,
but we know he'd be welcome here
to eat mountainous piles of greasy food
we slam fifty-two times a year.

We'll die of arterial sludge too soon.
We insult God's temple that way.
But never take one drop of wine,
though a few wrote that's what Jesus made.

Our yoke is easy, our burden light.
Repent! Yet get dirty looks.
If you are on your second wife,
we've our second set of books.

For divorce is bad, but murder good
in the ranking of our works.
Like God's our opinion is mighty low
of "Oh-ye-deevorced" jerks.

We open the bobble once each week,
otherwise gluttony, gossip, TV.
I know Christ didn't die for your sins, just for
self-ordained, self-righteous persons like me.

39 Social Poems   Ed Mikulski

THE SCHOOL CROSSING GUARD

The crossing guard he waits at school.
He's up before the dawn
to walk the children across the street.
On his face there's never a yawn.

For his job is so important
to those with loved ones in school.
They're learning about science, computers,
and math, English comp and the golden rule.

Each day at 7 and again at 3,
he begins his twice-daily pace.
And those little ones who trust in him
walk with confidence on their face.

To them he is the grandfatherly one
who stands so tall and proud.
He stops those cars with just one glance,
no need to shout out loud.

The kids he encourages and corrects.
He makes them toe the line.
If his wishes were to all come true,
they'd each of them turn out fine.

He prays that they will all be well
in the arena that is life. And God,
we hope, answers each of the prayers
of the crossing guard and his wife.

THE FAMILY VALUES CIRCUIT

I went to see the kids in Carolina
and with my son's brood hoping to connect
so that's where tithes they're going to collect
and caring, handsome preachers are thought finer.

Then on to Philly 'tween the bar and diner
by dear ones deemed sufficiently correct
our chuckling 'bout my apathy direct.
Could be I'm nine parts ostrich, one part whiner.

Then o'er to Jersey for my cousin's lecture,
reading "Methodist Thought for the Day"
and then that look
like he's the deacon, I in his prefecture
he'd quote all the Bible, just too big a book.
What my tall mom would say is now conjecture,
who seemed as virtuous but no hard stance took.

A VERY LONG PASS INTO THE END ZONE

What of the 77% of people who
picked the wrong one
of over 20 arguments, since born in
Alabama or Mexico or Iran?
Or Mongolia or Mumbai or
Tel Aviv or Hokkaido or Moscow?

So how about smoking just 7 percent,
or point seven percent,
or less, of 110-or-so-I.Q. jokers who
fell in love with their own totally
culture-based opinions over all others?
Can those egos be taken more lightly?
This is as father Abraham successfully begged
in Genesis 18. Well?

THE FARMER'S GARDEN

A country farmer created
a little garden patch
of small flowers growing
in a ten by five foot stretch
by the farmer's wife's house.

They were a gift to her –
each year came bachelor buttons
and zinnias, snap dragons and daisies,
wild little flowers, but each one
lovely, some even fragrant.

In the late-April garden
when the first black thunder clouds
gathered and thickened the air,
there were grander flowers yet.

Like pink and white peony puffs,
tulips of every hue,
white and tiger lilies,
and the first buds of purple lilacs.

Grander than all the wild roses
that were pink and white
and growing in patches on the bank,
was the great big bush of deep red roses
placed in a center space of honor.

So the farmer's wife sat
and glided with her husband
on the green garden glider at dusk,
on the comfortable lawn
beneath the 7-foot high bridal wreath bush
with flares of branches growing
countless white blossoms.

The farmer couple loved sitting
in the garden. They loved each other there.
They planned for more colorful flowers like poppies,
and humble ones like marigolds.

The flowers in that place were
each one loved, and watered and weeded
and smiled and shined on,
never picked, never cut, never trampled.

From my favorite poet, Shel Silverstein:

Many Leaves

One Tree

www.ingramcontent.com/pod-product-compliance
Lightning Source LLC
Chambersburg PA
CBHW070551300426
44113CB00011B/1871